DiscoverRoo
An Imprint of Pop!
popbooksonline.com

The Eras of Taylor Swift

THE TAYLOR SWIFT era

Track List

1. Tim McGraw
2. Picture To Burn
3. Teardrops On My Guitar
4. A Place in this World
5. Cold As You
6. The Outside
7. Tied Together with a Smile
8. Stay Beautiful
9. Should've Said No
10. Mary's Song (Oh My My My)
11. Our Song

by Elizabeth Andrews

This book is filled with videos, puzzles, games, and more! Scan the QR codes* while you read, or visit the website below to make this book pop.

popbooksonline.com/Debut

abdobooks.com

Published by Pop!, a division of ABDO, PO Box 398166, Minneapolis, Minnesota 55439.

Printed in the United States of America, North Mankato, Minnesota.

082025
012026

Cover Photo: Alexandra Tarasova (BigArtLab); Shutterstock

Interior Photos: AP Images; Flickr/Joe Haupt; Getty Images; Shutterstock Images, ZUMA Press, Inc/Alamy Stock Photo

Editor: Grace Hansen and Anna Schwartz

Series Designer: Laura Graphenteen

Library of Congress Control Number: 2025941001

Publisher's Cataloging-in-Publication Data

Names: Andrews, Elizabeth, author.

Title: The Taylor Swift era / by Elizabeth Andrews

Description: Minneapolis, Minnesota : Pop!, 2026 | Series: The eras of Taylor Swift | Includes online resources and index

Identifiers: ISBN 9781098248765 (lib. bdg.) | ISBN 9781098249281 (ebook)

Subjects: LCSH: Swift, Taylor, 1989- --Juvenile literature. | Popular music--Juvenile literature. | Popular (Songs, etc.)--Juvenile literature. | Albums--Juvenile literature. | Concerts--Juvenile literature. | Mass media and music--Juvenile literature.

Classification: DDC 782.42164101--dc23

*Scanning QR codes requires a web-enabled smart device with a QR code reader app and a camera.

TABLE OF CONTENTS

CHAPTER 1

TAYLOR'S FIRST SINGLE

On June 19, 2006, Taylor Swift released her very first **single**, "Tim McGraw." She was only 16 years old! Little did young Taylor know, she was on her way to change music history forever. But even then, she believed in herself.

WATCH A VIDEO HERE!

Meet Taylor

Birthday: December 13, 1989
Star Sign: Sagittarius
Place of Birth: West Reading, PA
Favorite Number: 13
Favorite Color: Purple
Favorite Meal: Chicken tenders and a chocolate shake

Two years before "Tim McGraw" was released, 14-year-old Taylor and her mother left their home in Pennsylvania for Nashville, Tennessee. They moved so Taylor could chase her dream of becoming a country music star.

Taylor's mother, Andrea, has always believed Taylor can accomplish anything she dreams of.

Nashville is known as the home of country music.

Taylor Swift and her mother spent months running around Nashville. They handed out CDs with songs written and performed by Taylor to different **labels**. Taylor performed whenever she could. Finally, at the famous Bluebird Cafe, Scott Borchetta heard Taylor on stage and knew he needed her on his label. He quickly **signed** Taylor Swift to Big Machine Records.

Taylor Swift sang the National Anthem at a 76ers basketball game when she was 11 years old.

Taylor was inspired to write "Tim McGraw" in math class. Her boyfriend was leaving for college, and she knew they would have to break up. "Tim McGraw" is about keeping happy memories even when something ends. After school, she went to the **studio** and sat down at the piano. She wrote the entire song in 15 minutes.

LIZ ROSE

Liz Rose is a country music songwriter. She started working with Taylor while she was writing for her first album. Liz co-wrote 7 of the 11 songs on the album, including the first single, "Tim McGraw." Taylor wrote with Liz on her second album too!

The "Tim McGraw" music video was released on July 22, 2006.

CHAPTER 2

SELF TITLED

Taylor's first **single** was very well received. Her new fans were excited for an entire album. On October 24, 2006, *Taylor Swift* was released to the world. It had 11 tracks, all written or co-written by Taylor. *Taylor Swift* sold 40,000 copies during its first week of sales.

EXPLORE LINKS HERE!

Some Swifties call the era of Taylor's first album "Debut Era."

DID YOU KNOW?

A deluxe version of *Taylor Swift* was released in November 2006 with three extra songs.

Taylor's **debut** album blended country and pop, which let younger fans connect to her music. Usually, country music fans were older. People told Taylor she was too young for the **genre**. They thought her career may be short if she started too early. They were wrong!

People were impressed by how talented of a songwriter Taylor was. The album was filled with emotional

Taylor Swift sang "Tim McGraw" to the man himself at an award show in 2007.

Taylor Swift was produced by Nathan Chapman. Taylor would work with him for a long time.

and honest lyrics about things most teenagers could relate to. The themes revolved around love, friendship, and **insecurities**. Taylor has said that writing music helped her when she felt like an outsider in high school.

Hidden Message

Taylor Swift hid messages in her debut lyric booklet. She would capitalize letters in the lyrics to spell out phrases. These were her first Easter eggs!

Besides "Tim McGraw," *Taylor Swift* had four other singles. They were "Teardrops On My Guitar," "Our Song," "Picture To Burn," and "Should've Said No." "Our Song" was the first of Taylor's songs to hit #1 on the country music charts and earned the Country Music Television (CMT) Award for Best Music Video!

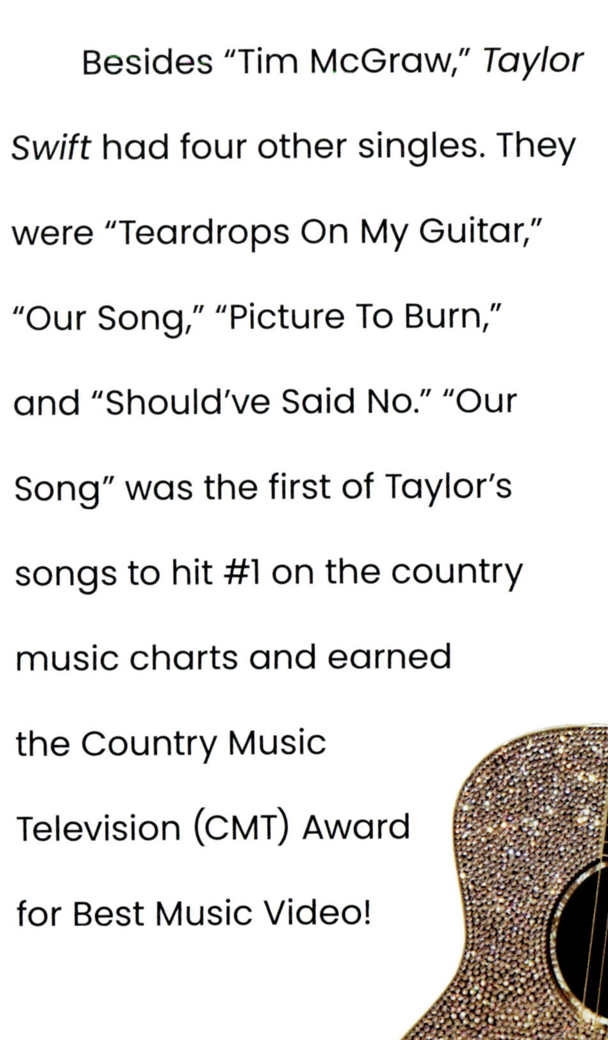

Taylor Swift played her sparkly guitar in the "Our Song" music video.

Taylor wore the same dress from her "Teardrops On My Guitar" music video to the 2007 CMT Music Awards.

CHAPTER 3

BEHIND THE LYRICS

Fans and music professionals have always loved Taylor Swift's songwriting. Her **debut** album brought forth Swifties' favorite activity—studying her song lyrics. Listeners want to know who or what she is singing about. There are three types of songs on *Taylor Swift*.

COMPLETE AN ACTIVITY HERE!

Taylor Swift fans didn't originally call themselves "Swifties." It wasn't until 2012 that Taylor used the term herself.

At the 2008 Academy of Country Music Awards, Taylor performed "Should've Said No" and made it rain on stage!

"Picture To Burn," "Should've Said No," and "Cold As You" are songs Taylor used to express anger. "Picture To Burn" is about a guy Taylor liked who made her mad. This is the first song in which Taylor admits to getting a bit **obsessive** about boys she has crushes on. "Should've Said No" is about an ex-boyfriend of Taylor's who **betrayed** her. This song is a lesson in making better choices.

"A Place in this World," "The Outside," and "Tied Together with a Smile" are songs about people trying to figure out who they are. In all three songs, the subjects feel different from those around them. "A Place in this World" was written after Taylor moved to Nashville. She was feeling lost and unsure about fitting into the music scene.

Taylor didn't have a debut set during the Eras Tour, but she sang songs from the album during her surprise set.

"Tim McGraw," "Teardrops On My Guitar," "Stay Beautiful," "Mary's Song (Oh My My My)," and "Our Song" are classic country love songs. Many young fans connected with "Teardrops On My Guitar" because it was about liking someone who just doesn't feel the same.

Taylor performed "Our Song" at the 2007 CMA Awards.

CHAPTER 4

FINDING HER PLACE IN THE WORLD

Since this was Taylor's first album, she did not headline a tour for it. Instead, she traveled as the opening act for other musicians. Musicians who headline tours often bring along one or two more artists to play sets before they take the stage.

Taylor got her first opening gig after another musician was fired from the Rascal Flatts' tour for playing too long.

In 2013, Strait, Keith Urban, and Paisley (from left to right) presented Taylor with an award.

Taylor opened for Tim McGraw, Faith Hill, George Strait, Rascal Flatts, and Brad Paisley on their tours. By opening for these big stars, Taylor got to play in front of all their fans every night. She gained tens of thousands of new fans through these tours.

Pickler became famous after being on the show American Idol.

DID YOU KNOW?

Taylor met her good friend Kellie Pickler when she toured with Brad Paisley.

Taylor played the Stagecoach Music Festival in 2008.

Taylor Swift also went on a long radio tour to **promote** her **debut** album. Taylor aimed to travel to 2,500 radio stations across the country. She slept in the back of a car as her mom drove them. On these radio stations, Taylor got to have fun with hosts and show off her personality. Listeners got to know her both as a person and an artist.

Taylor went from 32,000 friends on MySpace in 2006 to over 650,000 friends in 2008!

Even before having her own tour, Taylor found ways to connect with her fans. The old social media platform MySpace was her favorite place to do this. On MySpace she posted photos from her life as an opener, chatted with her fans, and let them know when new music and videos were being released. She told her fans to ask for her music on their radio stations. They helped her career blow up!

Taylor Swift enjoys playing small shows where she can connect with her fans.

MAKING CONNECTIONS

TEXT-TO-SELF

What is your favorite song from the *Taylor Swift* Era? Why is it your favorite?

TEXT-TO-TEXT

Have you read books about any other music artists? How are they similar to or different from Taylor Swift?

TEXT-TO-WORLD

Taylor Swift released her first single when she was 16! With the help of an adult, look up another musician who released music when they were in their teens. Write a few sentences about how they are similar to and different from Taylor.

GLOSSARY

betray — to not remain loyal or faithful.

debut — to appear for the first time, or the first appearance.

genre — a type of music. Country, rock, and jazz are examples of music genres.

insecurity — lack of confidence in oneself.

label — a company that helps make and release music recordings.

obsessive — overly interested in something.

promote — to help move forward.

sign — to agree to work with a company.

single — a song that is released as a stand-alone from the album.

studio — a place where recordings are made.

INDEX

DiscoverRoo!
ONLINE RESOURCES

This book is filled with videos, puzzles, games, and more! Scan the QR codes* while you read, or visit the website below to make this book pop.

popbooksonline.com/Debut

*Scanning QR codes requires a web-enabled smart device with a QR code reader app and a camera.